Starting Seeds Indoors

Ann Reilly

CONTENTS

Why Grow Plants from Seed?

In today's busy world, many of us look for the easiest and quickest way to achieve a goal. Buying plants at the nursery is a fast and simple way to get a garden growing. Why bother starting your own plants from seed? There are several reasons you might want to do so.

Each year, seed companies introduce new annuals with larger or more colorful flowers and vegetables with more luscious fruit. You may want to try new perennials from faraway places — or perhaps you have an "old-time" favorite. It's not always possible to find nursery plants of these varieties, and if you want to have them you must grow them from seed.

Growing your own plants from seed is more economical, a serious consideration if you have a large garden.

Some plants do well *only* when grown from seed. These include some annuals, like California poppy, sunflower, sweet pea and nasturtium, and vegetables such as beets, carrots, radishes and peas.

Children may be introduced to gardening by growing their own seedlings. Watching them witness the wonder of "creation" is a reward in itself.

And, finally, there is a certain satisfaction, come July, to look around a thriving garden and know that you were responsible for starting these plants from the very beginning.

Before You Germinate

What Is a Seed?

Seeds are produced by flowers and are the result of the joining of the male and female flower parts. The male part of the flower is known as the *stamen* and is made up of the *anther* and the *filament*. The anthers contain the pollen which is transferred to the female part of the flower, where fertilization takes place. This female part is called the *pistil* and is made up of the *stigma*, the *style*, and the *ovary*.

After fertilization (also called pollination) takes place, the seeds grow in the ovary until they ripen and can be harvested. Pollination is achieved by insects, the wind or by hand.

When differences occur naturally within a species, these are known as *varieties*. Those that are man-made are called *cultivars* (which stands for cultivated varieties). *Hybrids* are crosses between selected parents, and improvements of them. When choosing seed, it is important to study hybrids carefully to select the exact flower color or shape and type of vegetable that best suits your preferences and growing conditions.

Hybrids are valued for their increased flowering, uniformity, flower size, productivity or disease resistance. They are more expensive than open-pollinated seeds because of the cost of research and production; many seeds, such as those of petunias and impatiens, are greenhouse produced, and pollination is done by hand.

Since hybrids are crosses between two different parents, it is important not to save seeds from hybrid plants as they will not grow into the same plant and will usually be inferior. Seeds from non-hybrids, however, can be saved and grown the following season.

The outside of the seed is called the seed coat; its purpose is to encase the other parts and offer protection. With some seeds, such as lupines, sweet peas and false indigo, the seed coat is very hard and must be softened or nicked for germination to occur.

Inside the seed is the embryo, which is a small dormant plant, and the endosperm, which is a food source the plant uses during germination and in early stages of growth. The lower part of the embryo becomes the root, the upper part the growing tip, and in the center is (are) the cotyledon(s). Cotyledons are the first signs of growth, although they are not true leaves.

In order for a seed to germinate, it must be mature and viable, and receive the proper combination of moisture, temperature, light and air. When these requirements are met in the proper amount and order, the embryo grows, the seed coat bursts, the roots anchor, and the top begins to develop.

Special Treatments

Most annuals, vegetables and herbs germinate easily without a lot of fuss; a few, however, need special help. Perennial seeds, in general, need more attention than others. The reasons for this are varied: the seed coat may be too hard, preventing moisture from getting through; the embryo may be dormant; the seed might contain a chemical substance that inhibits germination; or it may need either complete darkness or constant light to germinate. Fortunately there are ways to deal with these various conditions. A list of seeds requiring special treatment begins on page 19.

Soaking. The soaking of seeds before sowing may be necessary for two reasons: to soften a hard seed coat, and to leach out chemicals that could inhibit germination. Place seeds in hot, but not boiling, water (190°F). For maximum contact of the seeds with the water, place the seeds in a shallow dish and cover them with 2–3 times their depth in water. Soaking for twenty-four hours will usually be long enough, but if instructions or experience dictate that a longer time is necessary, change the water once a day. After the soaking period, sow the seeds immediately and don't let them dry out.

Soaking is also a trick to speed up the germination of slow-to-germinate seeds. The embryo absorbs moisture, which gives the seed a head start on germination.

Scarification. Hard seed coats prevent or slow down the absorption of water and therefore germination. Scarification is the breaking of the seed coat by nicking it with a file, sandpaper, or a small scissor. Be careful not to cut too deeply into the seed coat so you don't damage the embryo.

When seeds are too small to be handled, soften the hard seed coat by soaking the seeds in water as described above.

On page 20 is a list of seeds that need to be scarified.

Stratification. Some seeds, particularly perennials, have an immature or dormant embryo when they are harvested. The seeds must be subjected to a moist-cold treatment before they are sown; this process is known as stratification. Lettuce and delphinium seeds become dormant if they are stored at a temperature over 75°F for more than a few weeks and must be chilled in order to germinate.

To stratify, mix the seeds with two to three times their volume in moistened sowing medium and place them either in the freezer or refrigerator.

You could also sow the seeds directly in their sowing flats and place the entire flats in the freezer or refrigerator, but this would take up more room.

Stratification will not work if the seeds are chilled in the packet or in water; seeds treated this way may never germinate. On page 21 is a list of seeds that require stratification. In general, seeds require six weeks to three months to stratify.

Stratification can also be done outdoors, provided your winter temperature drops to at least 40°F. You can sow the seeds either in the ground or in flats; if you do the latter, place the flats in a cold frame or on the north side of the house, away from drying winds and sun. Sink the flats into the ground up to their top. Seeds will germinate in the spring if placed outdoors in the fall. It takes longer this way, but often works better.

What You'll Need to Get Started

You need seeds, of course, and you'll also need a few more supplies to be successful at starting plants from seed.

Containers. Basically, anything that can hold media and is the right size can be used as a container to germinate seeds. There are many types of containers commercially available that are easy to use and reuse.

Seed-sowing flats should be about 3 to 3½ inches deep and can be of any size, depending on how many seeds you intend to germinate. Generally the ones you buy are made of plastic or fiber. The fiber ones are not as good as the plastic ones since they cannot be sterilized and therefore should not be reused. They also dry out more quickly. On the other hand, their porosity ensures good aeration, so they do have advantages.

Peat pots are good for seeds that resent transplanting, and for larger seeds. These pots are round or square, usually 2½ to 3 inches across, and are a combined germinating-growing-transplanting unit. Seeds are sown directly into the pot, and then later the pot is planted along with the plant. Peat pots are also useful for transplanting seedlings sown in flats.

Peat pellets, the most popular being the Jiffy products, are made of compressed peat. When placed in water they expand into a germination-growing-transplanting unit, similar in idea to the peat pot. They are best for larger, reliably germinating seeds and seeds that resent transplanting.

To keep peat pots and pellets properly watered and protected, place them in a plastic tray or container.

A new germinating method uses what are known as plugs, which are cone- or cylinder-shaped transplants. You can buy plug trays, which may have up to 200 plug holes. The holes are filled with medium, and one seed is sown into each plug. The unit goes from germination to transplanting without disturbing the roots.

You can make your own containers from things lying about the kitchen, such as coffee cans, paper cups, aluminum baking trays, milk or juice containers or plastic food storage containers. Before you use them, wash them well with soap and water and rinse them in a bleach solution (1 ounce or ⅛ cup bleach per 2 gallons water) to prevent diseases that might kill your seedlings.

Containers have two basic requirements in addition to cleanliness. The container should be 3 to 3½ inches deep for proper root development. Less than that and the roots will not have enough room to grow and will dry out too quickly. Deeper containers waste medium and serve no purpose.

Containers must also have excellent drainage. Purchased containers will already have drainage holes in the bottom. If you make your own containers, be sure to punch out some drainage holes in the bottom.

Germinating Media. No one perfect germinating medium exists, but some are better than others. Let's take a look at the components of germinating media to decide which is best.

Peat. Baled or bagged peat moss sold in the garden centers consists of partially decomposed aquatic plants, and its composition varies greatly. It can range from very acidic to almost neutral. Peat moss has a high water holding capacity and contains some nitrogen (about 1%), one of the elements necessary for plant growth. Peat moss is rarely used by itself for any type of propagating or growing, since water may not penetrate it easily or evenly. Also, it does not have good drainage or aeration qualities by itself. It is, however, a widely used component in sowing and growing mixtures.

Sphagnum moss. Sphagnum moss is harvested from bogs and dried. It is relatively sterile, lightweight, and able to absorb ten to twenty times its weight in water. It is generally milled (shredded) for use as a seed sowing medium. Its fertilizer value is low, so weak fertilizer solutions must be used with it after seedlings emerge. Because it is very acidic (pH 3.5), it can inhibit 'damping-off' — a fungus disease that can occur in cool, wet, early spring soils, and destroy young seedlings.

For years milled sphagnum moss was recommended as the best germination medium, to be used by itself. Unfortunately, it has some drawbacks — it is very difficult to moisten evenly and it often cakes when drying out. It has now given way to more desirable mixtures, some of which contain sphagnum moss.

Vermiculite. Vermiculite is expanded mica and has the capacity to hold tremendous amounts of water for long periods of time. Although it is not usually used alone for seed germination, it is an excellent addition to a mix because it is light and sterile. Its pH is neutral, it holds nutrients well, provides good aeration, and contains a high percentage of magnesium and potassium, two elements necessary for good root growth.

Perlite. Gray-white perlite is a volcanic ash that does not absorb water but holds water on its surface. It contains no essential elements and does not hold nutrients, but is valuable as a component in a germinating mix because it is light, sterile, and promotes good aeration. Like vermiculite, its pH is neutral.

Perlite stays cool and, therefore, is good in mixes used for germinating seeds that prefer lower temperatures. Its main disadvantage is that it will float to the surface when the seed bed is watered. It comes in various sizes; for seed germinating, use the finest kind.

Sand. Coarse builder's sand is often recommended for rooting cuttings, but it is not a good choice for seed sowing. It is heavy, contains no essential elements, does not hold nutrients, and is far from sterile. Stay away from it!

Soil. Soil from the garden should not be used to germinate seeds. It is usually not of the right texture to provide proper drainage and aeration, and seedlings might drown in it.

If soil must be used, it should be sterilized to kill the large number of weed seeds, insects and fungi that may be present. Bake it in a shallow pan in the oven, holding a temperature of 180°F for thirty minutes. Use a meat thermometer to make sure the temperature's right. Be prepared! This process emits an unpleasant odor. Commercial growers sterilize soil with chemicals, but this method is not recommended for amateur growers.

Mixtures. The best media for germinating seeds are sterile, soilless mixtures of peat or sphagnum moss with vermiculite and/or perlite. You can make these yourself, using from ⅓ to ½ sphagnum or peat moss, with the remainder vermiculite or perlite or a combination of the two. Experiment and choose the combination that works best.

The easiest way to obtain your germinating medium is to buy it ready-made. Many are available that are a combination of peat or sphagnum moss with vermiculite and/or perlite and enough fertilizer to get the seedlings off to a good start. This same mix can be used for transplanting and growing in containers.

The "perfect medium" has 50 percent solid material, 25 percent air spaces (in which roots grow and obtain necessary oxygen), and 25 percent moisture. A good mix is light, sterile, and firm but airy. It drains properly, yet retains the right amount of moisture for plant development. It helps eliminate damping-off, reduces the need for constant watching and expert judgment, promotes ideal growth, and lets you grow even the most difficult plants from seeds.

Environmental Conditions

Germination Temperature. Correct temperature is one of the environmental conditions critical for seed germination. While most seeds require temperatures of 70 to 75°F to germinate, some require cooler temperatures. See page 20 for a list of these.

Although the temperature in the room of a house may be 70°F, the medium in the germinating flat will be lower because it cools down as the surface moisture evaporates. To keep the medium at 70°F or above, gentle bottom heat is recommended. This heat may be obtained from a warm spot, such as on top of the refrigerator, or from a heating cable or heating tray.

Heating cables and trays may be spread out wherever seeds are germinated, whether it be on a windowsill or countertop or under fluorescent lights, with the germinating containers placed on top of them. They will heat flats to 70–75°F. When the flat gets warm enough (add a thermometer to your equipment list), simply pull the plug. Some have a built-in thermostat which automatically turns the system on and off. Waterproof soil heating cables may also be used in outdoor beds and cold frames.

If seeds are germinated indoors during the heat of summer, room temperatures will probably go high enough so that heating cables and heating trays will not be necessary (unless the house is air conditioned).

When cool temperatures are required, germinate the seeds indoors in an unheated garage, attic, basement, or porch which must, of course, have a source of natural or artificial light. Outdoors, this temperature is achieved in early spring or fall. Sow directly into seed beds, or set the flats outside in a spot protected from sun and wind, or in a cold frame.

Moisture and Humidity. Moisture and humidity are also critical. The germinating medium must be kept evenly moist, but never soaking wet. If there is too little moisture, germination will not occur; too much and the seeds will rot. If a good medium is used, watered thoroughly, and allowed to drain for several hours before sowing, the moisture level should be "perfect."

It is best to slip your seed flats into plastic bags or cover them with glass until the seeds germinate. This will keep the level of moisture and humidity just right, so the seed flats will not have to be watered often, if at all, before germination. This will eliminate the problems caused by overwatering, forgetfulness, or accidentally dislodging tiny seeds before they germinate.

Light. The final environmental factor, but one equally as important as the others, is light. Some seeds require light to germinate, while others need a complete absence of it to sprout. If light is needed for germination, the solution is not to cover the seeds. If darkness is necessary, cover the seeds completely with medium, unless they are too fine to be covered. In that instance, place the seed flats in total darkness or cover them with a material like newspaper or black plastic to block out the light until germination occurs. See pages 19 and 20 for a list of seeds that need darkness or light to germinate.

Once germinated, all seedlings need ample light to develop into strong, healthy plants. In fact, seedlings have the highest light intensity requirements of all plants. Using fluorescent lights or growing seedlings in a greenhouse is best, but if you do not have these available, an unshaded south window will do well.

Light is necessary to enable the plants to convert water and carbon dioxide into sugar (its food) in a process known as photosynthesis. If the light intensity is too low, which often happens during the short days of winter or prolonged cloudy periods, the plants will be unhealthy, tall and spindly.

Other Needs. There are a few other supplies needed to make seed germinating successful. *Labels* are very important, for no matter how good your memory is, you can't possibly remember which seed is in what flat, or when it was sown. Heavy white plastic markers are widely used, for they are durable and reusable. You can write on them in pencil, and your markings will stay there until you erase or wash them off. Keep them with your plants after you've moved them into the garden for your own information or in case a friend asks about a certain plant or variety. If you have good success with a variety, you'll want to know what it is so you can grow it again.

Young seedlings have to be watered carefully so they don't become damaged or dislodged. You can either water the plants from the bottom or with a *mister.*

A *record book* is a last good "extra." If you keep records this year, you'll appreciate being able to double-check next year on what you planted, when, how long it took to germinate, whether you started it too early or too late, and whether you grew too few or too many of a particular plant.

Now that you have everything together, it's time to sow. Read on!

While You Germinate

The type of seed you are going to germinate and grow determines when the seeds should be sown and how they should be handled. *Annuals* are plants that grow, flower, set seed, and complete their life cycle the same year the seeds are sown. *Biennials* have a two-year life cycle; seeds sown this year will flower next year and then set their seeds and die. Most vegetables are annuals and are sown and harvested in the same year. Herbs may be annuals or *perennials.* Most perennials die to the ground each winter and come back each spring, living for varying numbers of years, depending on the genus and/or species.

Annuals are started indoors or in seed beds outdoors, depending on the type of plant. Most are *frost-tender,* and should not be set in place outside until all danger of frost has passed (this date may be determined by your local County Agent). Some annuals are *hardy,* which means they may be sown in early spring as soon as the soil may be worked, and will not be killed by frost. A complete listing of hardy annuals is on page 21.

Vegetables, like annuals, are started either indoors or outdoors in spring, depending on the type of plant and how much time it requires before harvesting. Annual herbs are started like other annuals and vegetables, while perennial herbs are grown like other perennials.

Biennials and perennials are started in spring or summer up to two months before frost so the plants will be of sufficient maturity to be transplanted into their permanent location before cold fall weather sets in. Perennials requiring stratification are often sown outdoors in late fall or early winter for spring germination.

Sowing Seeds Indoors

Why start seeds indoors? There are a number of reasons. Many annuals and vegetables have such a long growing season that they won't flower or fruit if they don't get a head start indoors, especially in the north. Others may not need to be started indoors, but will flower or be productive for a much longer time if started early. Plants with fine seeds should be started indoors to protect them from the ravages of weather. Indoor seed starting eliminates worrying about weeds, insects, diseases, and excessive heat. When intercropping, you'll make more productive use of your land if you start with plants instead of seeds.

Annuals that must be started indoors include begonia, coleus, geranium, impatiens, lobelia, African marigold, petunia, salpiglossis, salvia, browallia, ornamental pepper, vinca, gerbera, lobelia, monkey flower, cupflower, poor-man's orchid, wishbone flower, pansy, and verbena.

While many vegetables are sown directly into the garden bed, others must be started indoors since the growing season, in all but the warmest parts of the country, is not long enough for them to produce. These include broccoli, brussels spouts, cabbage, cauliflower, celery, eggplant, leeks, okra, peppers, and tomatoes. Lettuce, onions, and melons are often started indoors as well.

Containers and Media. Start your sowing process by assembling your containers and making sure they are clean and have drainage holes.

If the container is made of fiber or peat, it must be soaked thoroughly before medium is placed in it or it will act as a wick and pull moisture out of the medium later on. Fill the container with water and allow it to absorb all that it can, draining off the rest, or place the flat or pot in a larger container of water until it has absorbed all it can. When the flat is thoroughly moistened, place a layer of stones or gravel in the bottom.

To judge how many seed flats to prepare, use this rule of thumb: A 5½" x 7½" flat will hold 100 seedlings from large seeds, 200 seedlings from medium seeds and 300 seedlings from fine seeds. Always sow about twice as many seeds as the number of plants you want since all of the seeds won't germinate, and some seedlings will be lost in the thinning and transplanting processes.

The container should be filled with premoistened sowing medium to within ¼ inch of the top. One of two methods may be used to moisten the medium. You can wet the medium in a plastic bag or a pot before placing it into the container (four cups of medium and one and one-half cups of water should be enough for one 5½"x 7½" flat), or put it in the container dry and let it draw up water from the bottom. Do this slowly so the medium won't separate. Dry medium is very difficult to evenly moisten with top watering. Once the medium is moist, make sure it is leveled out and patted down firmly, especially in the corners.

At this point, drench the sowing medium with a solution of benomyl fungicide (½ tablespoon per gallon of water) to prevent "damping-off" disease. The medium should be moist but not wet for sowing; if the medium is allowed to drain for approximately 2 hours after moistening and drenching, it should be perfect.

Fiber and peat containers and sowing medium should never be reused for seed sowing, for they may not be sterile. Any leftover medium from previous sowings can be used for transplanting or in containers.

If compressed peat pellets are to be used, soak them in water until they reach full size, which will take only minutes. These peat pellets or small peat pots should be used to sow and grow seeds that don't like to be transplanted later on (see page 21 for a complete list). Sow two to four seeds per pellet or pot in case they all don't germinate; remove all but the strongest seedling as soon as they germinate.

Sowing. Gather together your seeds and double-check to see if they need any special treatment before sowing, such as soaking, scarification, or stratification. Check the time required to germinate and grow to the point where they are transplanted outdoors so that seeding is done at the proper time. If a seed is supposed to be started six to eight weeks before planting outdoors, don't start it four weeks or ten weeks before. Immature seedlings started too late will not be large or strong enough to move outside when it's time, and those started too early will be too tall, lanky, or mature to transplant well.

Seedlings are best transplanted all-green and not in bud or flower.

You may not want to sow all of the seeds in each packet, just in case something goes awry and you have to start all over again.

If you're sowing two types of seed in the same flat, be sure you pick ones that have the same temperature requirements and germinate in approximately the same length of time.

It is best to sow seeds in rows, as it makes transplanting easier, so make depressions the thickness of the seed in the top of the medium with a label or pencil. Very slight depressions are needed for fine seeds and those that need light to germinate, since they must not be covered by the medium.

Write the name of the plant and the date of sowing on a label.

Cut the seed packet open across the top. Sow the seeds as carefully and evenly as you can. You can hold the seed packet in one hand, squeeze it together slightly, and tap it gently with your finger or a pencil. A few seeds should fall out with each tap; if too many come out at one time, they may be separated with a pencil.

As an alternative, crease a piece of paper and transfer the seeds into it. Let the seeds roll out or tap the paper with a pencil. Plastic seed sowers may also be used; these are clear plastic tubes with a hole at one end. Larger seeds may be individually placed by hand; large, flat ones should be sown vertically in the flat to decrease their chances of rotting.

Some seeds, like those of petunias, impatiens, and begonias, are very fine and dusty, and extreme care must be taken that they are evenly spread over the sowing medium. This is the one case where broadcasting rather than sowing in rows might be necessary and more practical.

Be careful when sowing that seeds aren't planted too close together. Seedlings need room for root growth, light, and air circulation. In addition, transplanting later on of properly spaced seedlings will be easier and done with less damage.

Very fine seeds, such as snapdragon, petunia, ageratum, and begonia, should not be covered with medium after sowing, but merely pressed into the surface of the sowing medium with a pencil, label, or a very fine mist from a rubber bulb sprinkler. To germinate, seeds must be in contact with moistened medium, not air. All other seeds, except those that need light to germinate, should be covered with one or two times their thickness with dry sowing medium, and then watered carefully with a fine mist of room temperature water.

Rubber bulb sprinklers are recommended because they deliver a fine spray that will not dislodge the seeds.

Seeds that need light to germinate should not be covered with medium but merely pressed into contact with medium. Those seeds that need darkness, as long as they are not fine, should be completely covered with sowing medium. Fine seeds that need darkness to germinate are treated in one of two ways. Either place the flat in a dark spot until germination occurs, or cover the flat with black plastic or some other material to block the light until the seeds have sprouted.

The seed flat is now ready for germination. Place the entire flat into a plastic bag and tie it tightly, or cover the flat with a piece of glass or plastic. Either of these methods will keep the humidity high enough so that the seed flat should not need to be watered before germination, thereby reducing the chance of drowning or dislodging the seeds. When using a plastic bag or sheet, be sure it does not touch the top of the medium. Extra labels or toothpicks set at the corners of the flat will keep the plastic off the medium.

Pelleted Seed. Some very fine seeds, such as petunia, coleus, pinks and snapdragons, are sometimes *pelleted*, (coated) to make them easier to handle and space properly. The coating increases their size and protects the seed; generally these seeds germinate more reliably and quickly. Do not cover the pellets when sowing, but merely press them gently into the surface.

Germinating. Once your seed flat is ready, place it in a location where it will receive the proper light and temperature for seed germination. If you have an area in the house, such as a spare room, attic, or basement, where your seed garden would be out of sight and where a water spill or other accident wouldn't cause a problem, so much the better. If not, you can use the kitchen, den or bedroom — wherever you have the space. If you will be using a windowsill, it's wise to protect it from moisture.

With very few exceptions, seed flats should be placed in good light but not in direct sun while germination is taking place, or under fluorescent lights.

The use of a soil thermometer will ensure that the medium is the right temperature for germinating.

The germination times given in the tables on page 24 are average ones and may vary by 25 percent in either direction, depending on environmental factors. Don't give up too early if your seeds don't germinate. If, however, too much time has gone by, try to figure out what went wrong and start again.

Even though the glass or plastic covering on the seed flat should minimize the need for watering, check the medium once in a while to make sure it isn't drying out.

Condensation on the plastic or glass does not necessarily mean the flat has been overwatered; a change in temperature may cause moisture to form. Feel the medium to be sure. If it is too wet, leave the glass or plastic off for several hours to dry it a little, and then cover it again. Don't, however, let the medium dry out completely at any time.

Once the seeds have started to germinate, remove the plastic or glass from the seed flats. Gradually move the seedlings into full sun or strong light; sudden changes in light may injure tender seedlings.

Germinating under Lights. If you have the space, germinating seeds under lights is the more productive method. You won't have to worry about short and cloudy days or limited space on windowsills. Light gardens can be situated anywhere as long as electricity is nearby and the temperature is right.

You can purchase one of the many fluorescent lights available for indoor gardens, but since seedlings need light in the blue and green area of the spectrum to grow properly (yellow, orange and red wavelengths promote flowering), you can also use common household cool white lights.

Except for those seeds requiring darkness to germinate, place seedling flats under lights for twenty-four hours per day until germination occurs. After that, the light duration should be cut down to twelve to fourteen hours per day. Once the plants start to grow, the light source should be 3–6 inches above the top of the seedlings. To accomplish this, you'll need a system to either raise the lights or lower the shelves as the plants grow.

If the leaves turn downward or look burned during growth, the lights are too close. If the seedlings are starting to grow tall and spindly, the lights are too far away.

Seedling Care. In the following weeks, how you care for your seedlings is critical. Water, of course, is most important. The root systems of the new seedlings are not yet well developed, so the medium must always be kept moist, but never completely wet, or the seedlings will suffer from poor aeration. If the medium starts to lighten in color, that is a sign that it is drying out. Check every day to see if water is needed. Watering from the bottom is best until the seedlings reach a fairly good size, since watering from above can dislodge young plants or knock them over. If you do water from above, water the medium between the seedling rows.

Most plants will grow successfully at normal room temperatures of 60–70°F. Those that require cooler germination temperatures will usually like cooler growing temperatures as well.

If seedlings are grown on the windowsill or at the edge of the light garden, they should be turned regularly so they will grow straight and evenly.

Once the first true leaves have developed (the first growth you will see are the cotyledons, which are food storage cells), it is time to start fertilizing. No food is needed prior to this point, since the seedling is using food that was stored in the seed. Use a soluble plant food such as Hyponex, Miracle-Gro, or Peters at one-quarter the label strength when seedlings are small, increasing to one-half the label strength as the plant matures. It is better to fertilize with this weak solution once a week instead of feeding with full-strength solution once a month; growth will be more even and burning of the seedlings will be avoided. When bottom-watering young seedlings, mix the fertilizer into the water; later on, the seedlings can be fertilized from above.

Transplanting. It is possible to plant seedlings directly from the seed flat into the garden, but this is generally not advised. The seedlings should be transplanted to a larger container first or at least thinned so they will not be crowded, leggy, weak, or susceptible to damage. One transplanting is usually enough, and will guarantee good, strong root development and easier adjustment of the plant to the garden. Seedlings started in individual pots do not need to be transplanted.

After the seedlings have developed four true leaves, it is time to transplant or thin. If thinning, leave at least 1" between seedlings in the flat. Larger seedlings will need more space. These seedlings may now be left to grow until it is time to transplant them into the garden, although they will benefit from transplanting at this point into their own pots.

There's one interesting fact to be aware of when thinning or transplanting seedlings: the weakest seedlings in annual mixtures such as snapdragons and phlox often produce the most unusual colors and types. For a good balance, transplant all seedlings, large and small.

When transplanting, first water the seedlings thoroughly. Peat pots, pellets or small plastic pots are best for transplanting. If the seedlings are being transplanted into peat pots or flats, wet the containers as well, and don't forget to premoisten the medium to be used for transplanting. Seedlings can also be transplanted into flats; those with dividers or compartments lead to more compact root development and easier transplanting, without shock to the roots.

You may use the same medium you used for germinating for transplanting, or use leftover medium from previous seed sowings. It is not critical that medium for transplants be sterile.

Fill the container with pre-moistened medium to just below the top of the container. With a label or pencil, open a hole in the center of the medium, deep and wide enough to fit the seedling's roots.

Using a label, spoon handle, fork, or similar tool, gently lift the seedlings from the flat. Separate them carefully so as not to break any more roots than necessary. A small amount of medium should cling to the seedling's roots. Always handle a seedling by its leaves and NEVER by its stem; if damage is accidentally done, the seedling will grow a new leaf, but never a new stem.

Lower the seedling into the hole you made in the medium, placing it slightly deeper than it was growing in the seed flat, and gently press the medium around the roots. Don't forget to put a label in the container!

Peat pots and pellets should be set into an empty tray or flat to keep them intact and to catch excess water.

Transplants will often droop or wilt because they have lost some of their roots. They will recover quickly if properly cared for. Keep the transplants in good light but not full sun for several days, increasing the light intensity gradually. If you've transplanted during cloudy weather, the containers can go right onto the windowsill; if you grow under lights, the transplants can go under the fluorescents right away. If the plants become tall and spindly later on, they're not getting enough light.

Water when necessary, never allowing the transplants to wilt, and keeping the medium evenly moist but not soaking wet. Once a week, when watering, add soluble fertilizer at one-half the recommended label strength.

Several plants benefit from pinching while in the transplant stage. Single-stemmed plants such as snapdragons, dahlias, and chrysanthemums will be more bushy and colorful if pinched. Those that are getting too tall before the weather is right for outdoor planting should also be pinched. Simply reach into the center of the plant and nip out the growing tip.

Once roots show through the container walls, the plants are ready to be moved to the garden. If it's too early for outdoor planting, they may be held in the container for up to four weeks until the weather is right.

Hardening Off. One week before indoor-grown seedlings are shifted outdoors to the garden, start to harden them off. This process acclimates the soft and tender plants, which have been protected from wind, cool temperatures, and strong sun, and gradually gets them used to their new environment.

Move the trays or flats of potted plants outside into a sheltered, shady area such as a porch, cold frame or under a tree or shrub. If it gets cold at night, move them back inside. After two or three days, give them half a day of sun, increasing the exposure gradually to a full day. Make sure the transplants are well watered during this "hardening off" period. If at all possible, don't place transplants on the ground if slugs are a problem in your area.

After You Germinate

After your seeds have germinated and the seedlings are growing strong and healthy, it's time to plant them into the garden.

Planting into the Garden

Double-check planting dates before you start moving plants outside. Most annuals and vegetables must wait until danger of frost is past to be placed outside; some can go out earlier. Tomatoes, eggplant, and peppers should wait a little longer until the ground has completely warmed up.

Plan the garden in advance. Select plants for sun and shade, and check planting distances.

The soil must be well prepared in advance to get the most from your flowers, vegetables or herbs.

Before moving your plants into the garden, water both the ground outside and the transplants. This will cut down on transplanting shock. It's preferable to do your transplanting on a cloudy day or late in the afternoon so the heat of the sun won't cause excess wilting. If you've used individual peat pots or peat pellets, transplant shock and wilting will be held to a minimum.

Dig a hole about twice the size of the root ball. Set the transplant into the hole so the root ball will be covered by ¼ inch of soil, and press soil firmly about its roots so there is good contact between the soil and the roots.

Seedlings in peat pellets can be planted as they are. When planting a peat pot, peel whatever you can off the pot before planting so the walls of the pot will not confine the roots. Be sure the peat pot is completely covered with soil so it will not dry out and act as a wick, allowing moisture to escape from around the roots.

If your transplants have been growing in flats that are not compartmentalized, very carefully cut out a root ball with a knife or a trowel. If the transplants have been growing in individual plastic pots or flat compartments, turn them upside down and tap them on the bottom, and they will come out easily.

The newly-set-out plants may look a little sparse at first, but they will grow and fill in quickly, and you won't want them to be overcrowded. Adequate spacing also cuts down on disease.

Water well immediately after transplanting and again every day for about a week until the plants are well established and growing. Some transplants may wilt at first, but misting them every day or shading them will help them to quickly revive.

From this point on, a few simple maintenance practices will ensure a successful garden and a lot of enjoyment.

Frost Protection

If an unexpected late frost occurs after transplanting, you will need to protect your tender seedlings from frost damage. This can be done by placing Styrofoam cups or Hotkaps over the plant when frost threatens and removing them when the temperature warms up.

Seeds That Require Special Treatment

Seeds That Need Light to Germinate

Achillea species — YARROW; *Ageratum Houstonianum* — FLOSSFLOWER; *Alyssum montanum* — BASKET OF GOLD; *Anethum graveolens* — DILL; *Antirrhinum majus* — SNAPDRAGON; *Aquilegia* species and hybrids — COLUMBINE; *Arabis* species — ROCK CRESS, WALL CRESS; *Begonia* species — BEGONIA; *Brassica oleracea* Acephala — ORNAMENTAL CABBAGE; *Browallia speciosa* — BROWALLIA; *Campanula* species

— BELLFLOWER; *Capsicum annuum* — ORNAMENTAL PEPPER; *Chrysanthemum Parthenium* — MATRICARIA, FEVERFEW; *Chrysanthemum* x superbum — SHASTA DAISY; *Coleus* x *hybridus* — COLEUS; *Coreopsis grandiflora* — TICKSEED; *Doronicum cordatum* — LEOPARD'S-BANE; *Gaillardia* x *grandiflora* — BLANKET FLOWER; *Gerbera Jamesonii* hybrids — TRANSVAAL DAISY; *Helichrysum bracteatum* — STRAWFLOWER; *Impatiens Wallerana* — IMPATIENS; *Lactuca sativa* — LETTUCE; *Lobularia maritima* — SWEET ALYSSUM; *Lynchis chalcedonica* — MALTESE-CROSS; *Matthiola* species — STOCK; *Moluccella laevis* — BELLS-OF-IRELAND; *Nicotiana alata* — FLOWERING TOBACCO; *Papaver orientale* — ORIENTAL POPPY; *Petunia* x *hybrida* — PETUNIA; *Platycodon grandiflorus* — BALLOON FLOWER; *Primula* species except *P. sinensis* — PRIMROSE; *Reseda odorata* — MIGNONETTE; *Salvia* species — SALVIA (Red flowered varieties); *Sanvitalia procumbens* — CREEPING ZINNIA; *Satureja* species — SAVORY; *Tithonia rotundifolia* — MEXICAN SUNFLOWER.

Seeds That Need Darkness to Germinate

Borago officinalis — BORAGE; *Calendula officinalis* — POT MARIGOLD; *Catharanthus roseus* — PERIWINKLE; *Centaurea Cyanus* — BACHELOR'S-BUTTON; *Consolida ambigua* — LARKSPUR; *Coriandrum sativum* — CORIANDER; *Delphinium* species — DELPHINIUM; *Foeniculum* species — FENNEL; *Gazania rigens* — TREASURE FLOWER; *Lathyrus odoratus* — SWEET PEA; *Myosotis* species — FORGET-ME-NOT; *Nemesia strumosa* — NEMESIA; *Papaver* species except *P. orientale* — POPPY; *Phlox* species — PHLOX; *Primula sinensis* — CHINESE PRIMROSE; *Salpiglossis sinuata* — PAINTED-TONGUE; *Schizanthus* x *wisetonensis* —BUTTERFLY FLOWER, POOR-MAN'S ORCHID; *Tropaeolum majus* — NASTURTIUM; *Verbena* species — VERBENA; *Viola* species — VIOLA, VIOLET, PANSY.

Seeds That Require Soaking before Sowing

Abelmoschus esculentus — OKRA; *Armeria maritima* — THRIFT, SEA PINK; *Asparagus officinalis* — ASPARAGUS; *Hibiscus* species — MALLOW; *Ipomoea* species — MORNING-GLORY and other closely related plants; *Lathyrus latifolius* — PERENNIAL PEA; *Lathyrus odoratus* — SWEET PEA; *Liriope Muscari* — LILYTURF; *Lupinus* species — LUPINES; *Pastinaca sativa* — PARSNIPS; *Petroselinum crispum* — PARSLEY.

Seeds That Need Stratification before Sowing (cold treatment)

Angelica Archangelica — ANGELICA; *Aquilegia* species and hybrids — COLUMBINE; *Brassica oleracea* Acephala — ORNAMENTAL CABBAGE; *Dicentra spectabilis* — BLEEDING-HEART; *Dictamnus albus* — GAS PLANT; *Helleborus niger* — CHRISTMAS ROSE; *Hemerocallis* hybrids — DAYLILY; *Lavandula angustifolia* — LAVENDER; *Machaeranthera tanacetifolia* — TAHOKA DAISY; *Phlox paniculata* — PHLOX; *Primula* species — PRIMROSE; *Trillium ovatum* — WAKE-ROBIN; *Trollius europaeus* — GLOBEFLOWER; *Viola* species — VIOLA, VIOLET, PANSY.

Seeds That Must Be Scarified (nicked or filed) before Sowing

Baptisia australis — WILD BLUE INDIGO, FALSE INDIGO; *Hibiscus* species — MALLOW; *Ipomoea* species — MORNING GLORY and other closely related plants; *Lathyrus* species — PERENNIAL and SWEET PEA; *Lupinus* species — LUPINES.

Seeds That Need Cool Temperatures (55°F) to Germinate

Aubrieta deltoidea — FALSE ROCK CRESS, PURPLE ROCK CRESS; *Cheiranthus Cheiri* — WALLFLOWER; *Dictamnus albus* — GAS PLANT; *Erigeron* species —

MIDSUMMER ASTER, FLEABANE; *Eschscholzia californica* — CALIFORNIA POPPY; *Heuchera sanguinea* — CORALBELLS; *Iberis sempervirens* — CANDYTUFT; *Lathyrus latifolius* — PERENNIAL PEA; *Lathyrus odoratus* — SWEET PEA; *Matricaria recutita* — CHAMOMILE; *Moluccella laevis* — BELLS-OF-IRELAND; *Nemophila Menziesii* — BABY-BLUE-EYES; *Papaver* species — POPPY; *Penstemon* hybrids — BEARD-TONGUE; *Phlox Drummondii* — ANNUAL PHLOX; *Rosmarinus officinalis* — ROSEMARY; *Thymus* species — THYME, MOTHER OF THYME.

Seeds That Should Be Sown as Soon as Possible (They are not long-lived and should not be stored)

Angelica Archangelica — ANGELICA; *Chrysanthemum coccineum* — PYRETHRUM, PAINTED DAISY; *Delphinium* species — DELPHINIUM; *Dimorphotheca sinuata* — CAPE MARIGOLD; *Geranium sanguineum* — CRANESBILL; *Gerbera Jamesonii* hybrids — TRANSVAAL DAISY; *Kochia scoparia* — BURNING BUSH; *Salvia splendens* — SCARLET SAGE.

Hardy Annuals (Seeds that may be sown outdoors in early spring as soon as soil can be worked and will not be affected by late spring frosts)

Allium Ampeloprasum — LEEK; *Allium Cepa* — ONION; *Anethum graveolens* — DILL; *Anthriscus Cerefolium* — CHERVIL; *Arctotis* species and hybrids — AFRICAN DAISY; *Beta vulgaris* — BEET, SWISS CHARD; *Borago officinalis* — BORAGE; *Brassica* species — BROCCOLI, BRUSSELS SPROUTS, CABBAGE, CAULIFLOWER, CHINESE CABBAGE, COLLARDS, KALE, KOHLRABI, MUSTARD, TURNIP; *Centaurea Cyanus* — BACHELOR'S-BUTTON, CORNFLOWER; *Consolida ambigua* — LARKSPUR; *Coriandrum sativum* — CORIANDER; *Daucus Carota* var. *sativus* — CARROT; *Eruca vesicaria* — ROCKET; *Eschscholzia californica* — CALIFORNIA POPPY; *Gypsophila* species — BABY'S-BREATH; *Lactuca sativa* — LETTUCE; *Lepidium sativum* — GARDEN CRESS; *Lobularia maritim* — SWEET ALYSSUM; *Machaeranthera tanacetifolia* — TAHOKA DAISY; *Matricaria recutita* — CHAMOMILE; *Mentzelia Lindleyi* — BLAZING STAR; *Moluccella laevis* — BELLS-OF-IRELAND; *Nemophila Menziesii* — BABY-BLUE-EYES; *Origanum Majorana* — MARJORAM; *Pastinaca sativa* — PARSNIPS; *Petroselinum crispum* — PARSLEY; *Phlox Drummondii* — ANNUAL PHLOX; *Pisum sativum* — PEA; *Raphanus sativus* — RADISH; *Reseda odorata* — MIGNONETTE; *Spinacia oleracea* — SPINACH.

Seedlings That Resent Transplanting (Sow seeds where they are to grow or in individual pots)

Anethum graveolens — DILL; *Anthriscus Cerefolium* — CHERVIL; *Beta vulgaris* — SWISS CHARD, BEET; *Borage officinalis* — BORAGE; *Brassica* species — MUSTARD, RUTABAGA, TURNIP; *Carum Carvi* — CARAWAY; *Coriandrum sativum* — CORIANDER; *Daucus Carota* — CARROT; *Eruca vesicaria* — ROCKET; *Eschscholzia californica* — CALIFORNIA POPPY; *Foeniculum* species — FENNEL; *Lavatera* hybrids — TREE MALLOW; *Linum* species — FLAX; *Lupinus* species — LUPINE; *Nigella damascena* — LOVE-IN-A-MIST; *Papaver* species — POPPY; *Pastinaca sativa* — PARSNIP; *Petroselinum crispum* — PARSLEY; *Phlox Drummondii* — ANNUAL PHLOX; *Pimpinella Anisum* — ANISE; *Pisum sativum* — PEA; *Sanvitalia procumbens* — CREEPING ZINNIA; *Sesamum indicum* — SESAME; Spinacia oleracea — SPINACH; *Trachymene coerulea* — BLUE LACE FLOWER; *Tropaeolum majus* — NASTURTIUM; *Zea Mays* — CORN.

Species	Germination time in days	Indoor sowing — number of weeks before transplanting outdoors	Outdoor sowing — number of weeks before last frost	Outdoor transplanting — number of weeks before last frost	Planting distance in inches
Ageratum Houstonianum AGERATUM	5–10	6–8	last frost	last frost	9–12
Amaranthus species JOSEPH'S-COAT, LOVE LIES BLEEDING	10–15	3–4	last frost	last frost	12–24
Antirrhinum majus SNAPDRAGON	10–14	6–8	2	last frost	6–8
Arctotis stoechadifolia AFRICAN DAISY	21–35	6–8	4	4	10–12
Begonia semperflorens WAX BEGONIA	15–20	10–12	—	last frost	6–8
Brassica oleracea ORNAMENTAL KALE AND CABBAGE	10–18	6–8	—	first frost in fall	12–15
Browallia speciosa BROWALLIA	14–21	6–8	—	last frost	8–10
Calendula officinalis POT MARIGOLD	10–14	4–6	6	4	10–12
Callistephus chinensis CHINA ASTER	10–14	6–8	last frost	last frost	6–15
Capsicum annuum ORNAMENTAL PEPPER	21–25	6–8	—	last frost	6–8
Catharanthus roseus VINCA, PERIWINKLE	15–20	10–12	—	last frost	8–10
Celosia cristata CELOSIA, COCKSCOMB	10–15	4–6	last frost	last frost	6–12
Centaurea Cyanus BACHELOR'S-BUTTON	7–14	4–6	6	4	6–12
Chrysanthemum species ANNUAL CHRYSANTHEMUM	10–18	8–10	last frost	last frost	12–15
Cleome Hasslerana SPIDER FLOWER	10–14	4–6	last frost	last frost	24–30
Coleus X hybridus COLEUS	10–15	6–8	—	last frost	10–12
Consolida ambigua LARKSPUR	8–15				

Coreopsis tinctoria CALLIOPSIS	5-10	6-8	last frost	last frost	
Cosmos bipinnatus COSMOS	5-10	5-7	last frost	last frost	9-18
Dahlia hybrids DAHLIA	5-10	4-6	last frost	last frost	6-30
Dianthus species DIANTHUS, PINKS	5-10	8-10	last frost	last frost	6-12
Dimorphotheca sinuata CAPE MARIGOLD	10-15	4-5	last frost	last frost	6-8
Eschscholzia californica CALIFORNIA POPPY	10-12	—	4-6	—	6-8
Euphorbia species ANNUAL POINSETTIA / SNOW-ON-THE-MOUNTAIN	10-15	6-8	last frost	last frost	8-12
Gaillardia pulchella BLANKET FLOWER	15-20	4-6	last frost	last frost	8-12
Gazania ringens TREASURE FLOWER	8-14	4-6	last frost	last frost	8-12
Gerbera Jamesonii TRANSVAAL DAISY	15-25	8-10	—	last frost	10-12
Helianthus species SUNFLOWER	10-14	—	last frost	—	24-36
Helichrysum bracteatum STRAWFLOWER	7-10	4-6	last frost	last frost	9-12
Iberis species CANDYTUFT	10-15	6-8	last frost	last frost	6-8
Impatiens Balsamina BALSAM	8-14	6-8	last frost	last frost	10-12
Impatiens Wallerana IMPATIENS	15-20	10-12	—	last frost	8-12
Ipomoea species MORNING-GLORY	5-7	4-6	last frost	last frost	12-15
Kochia scoparia BURNING BUSH	10-15	4-6	last frost	last frost	15-18
Lathyrus odoratus SWEET PEA	20-30	—	6-8	—	12-15
Lavatera hybrids TREE MALLOW	15-20	—	4-6	—	18-24
Lobelia Erinus LOBELIA	15-20	10-12	—	last frost	4-6
Lobularia maritima SWEET ALYSSUM	8-15	4-6	4	2	5-8
Machaeranthera tanacetifolia TAHOKA DAISY	25-30	6-8	4-6	4-6	6-8
Matthiola incana STOCK	7-10	6-8	last frost	last frost	12-15
Mimulus species MONKEY FLOWER	8-12	10-12	—	2	6-8

Species	Germination time in days	Indoor sowing — number of weeks before transplanting outdoors	Outdoor sowing — number of weeks before last frost	Outdoor transplanting — number of weeks before last frost	Planting distance in inches
Mirabilis Jalapa FOUR-O'CLOCK	7–10	4–6	last frost	last frost	12–18
Moluccella laevis BELLS-OF-IRELAND	25–35	—	6–8	—	12–15
Nemesia strumosa NEMESIA	7–14	4–6	last frost	last frost	6–8
Nemophila Menziesii BABY-BLUE-EYES	7–12	—	6–8	—	6–9
Nicotiana alata FLOWERING TOBACCO	10–20	6–8	last frost	last frost	10–12
Nierembergia species CUPFLOWER	15–20	10–12	—	last frost	4–6
Pelargonium X hortorum GERANIUM	5–15	12–15	—	last frost	10–12
Petunia X hybrida PETUNIA	10–12	10–12	—	last frost	10–12
Phlox Drummondii ANNUAL PHLOX	10–15	—	6–8	—	6–8
Portulaca grandiflora ROSE MOSS	10–15	4–6	last frost	last frost	12–15
Reseda odorata MIGNONETTE	5–10	—	4–6	—	10–12
Salpiglossis sinuata PAINTED-TONGUE	15–20	6–8	—	last frost	8–12
Sanvitalia procumbens CREEPING ZINNIA	10–15	—	last frost	—	5–7
Schizanthus X wisetonensis POOR-MAN'S ORCHID	20–25	10–12	—	—	12–15
Tagetes erecta AFRICAN MARIGOLD	5–7	4–6	—	last frost	12–18
Tagetes patula FRENCH MARIGOLD	5–7	4–6	last frost	last frost	6–8
Thunbergia alata BLACK-EYED SUSAN VINE	10–15	6–8	last frost	last frost	10–12
Tithonia rotundifolia MEXICAN SUNFLOWER	5–10	6–8	last frost	last frost	24–30
Toremia Fournieri WISHBONE FLOWER					

ANNUALS

Tropaeolum majus NASTURTIUM	7–12	—	last frost	—	8–12
Verbena X *hybrida* VERBENA	20–25	12–14	—	last frost	6–8
Viola X *Wittrockiana* PANSY	10–20	6–8	—	4–6	4–6
Zinnia elegans ZINNIA	5–7	4–6	last frost	last frost	6–18

PERENNIALS

Achillea species YARROW	10–12	6–8	A	B	12–18
Alcea rosea HOLLYHOCK	10–14	6–8	A	B	18–36
Alyssum montanum BASKET OF GOLD	7–14	6–8	C	B	6–8
Anchusa azurea SUMMER FORGET-ME-NOT	14–21	6–8	A	B	18–30
Chrysanthemum coccineum PYRETHRUM, PAINTED DAISY	20–25	6–8	A	B	10–12
Chrysanthemum X *morifolium* GARDEN CHRYSANTHEMUM	7–10	6–8	C	F	8–18
Chrysanthemum Parthenium FEVERFEW	10–15	4–6	C	B	6–12
Chrysanthemum X *superbum* SHASTA DAISY	10–14	4–6	A	B	12–18
Coreopsis grandiflora TICKSEED	20–25	6–8	G	B	12–15
Delphinium species DELPHINIUM	8–15	6–8	A	B	12–24
Dicentra spectabilis BLEEDING HEART	30+	8–10	I	B	24–30
Dictamnus albus GAS PLANT	30–40	6–8	I	B	30–36
Digitalis species FOXGLOVE	15–20	6–8	A	B	15–24
Doronicum cordatum LEOPARD'S-BANE	15–20	6–8	A	B	12–15

Species	Germination time in days	Indoor sowing — number of weeks before transplanting outdoors	Outdoor sowing — number of weeks before last frost	Outdoor transplanting — number of weeks before last frost	Planting distance in inches
PERENNIALS					
Echinacea purpurea PURPLE CONEFLOWER	10–20	6–8	A	B	18–24
Erigeron species MIDSUMMER ASTER	15–20	6–8	D	B	10–12
Gaillardia X grandiflora BLANKET FLOWER	15–20	4–6	C	B	8–15
Geranium sanguineum CRANESBILL	20–40	8–10	C	B	10–12
Geum species AVENS	21–28	6–8	A	B	12–18
Gypsophila species BABY'S-BREATH	10–15	6–8	A	B	18–24
Helleborus niger CHRISTMAS ROSE	14–20	6–8	H	B	12–15
Hemerocallis hybrids DAYLILY	21–50	9–15	D	B	18–36
Heuchera sanguinea CORALBELLS	10–15	6–8	D	B	9–15
Hibiscus Moscheutos MALLOW	15–30	6–8	A	B	24–36
Hosta species PLANTAIN LILY	15–20	6–8	A	B	10–12
Iberis sempervirens CANDYTUFT	16–20	8–10	C	B	6–9
Kniphofia Uvaria RED-HOT-POKER, TRITOMA	10–20	6–8	C	B	18–24
Lathyrus latifolius PERENNIAL PEA	20–30	4–6	C	B	10–12
Liatris species GAY-FEATHER	20–25	6–8	A	B	12–15
Linum species FLAX	20–25	—	A	—	10–12
Liriope Muscari LILYTURF	25–30	8–10	J	B	6–12
Lunaria annua MONEY PLANT	10–14	6–8	C	F	12–15
Lupinus species LUPINE	20–25	6–8	C	B	18–24
Lychnis chalcedonica MALTESE-CROSS	21–25	6–8	A	B	

Lythrum Salicaria LOOSESTRIFE	15–20	6–8	C	b	10–24
Monarda didyma BEE BALM	15–20	4–6	A	B	12–15
Myosotis scorpioides FORGET-ME-NOT	8–14	6–8	I	B	8–12
Oenothera species EVENING PRIMROSE	15–20	6–8	J	B	6–12
Papaver species POPPY	10–15	—	D	—	12–18
Penstemon hybrids BEARD-TONGUE	20–30	8–10	D	B	12–18
Phlox paniculata PHLOX	25–30	8–10	I	B	24–36
Physostegia virginiana FALSE DRAGONHEAD	20–25	6–8	A	B	15–18
Platycodon grandiflorus BALLOON FLOWER	10–15	6–8	A	B	12–18
Polemonium caeruleum JACOB'S-LADDER	20–25	6–8	D	B	15–18
Primula species PRIMROSE	21–40	8–10	D	B	6–8
Rudbeckia hirta GLORIOSA DAISY	5–10	4–6	A	B	12–18
Santolina Chamaecyparissus LAVENDER COTTON	15–20	6–8	A	B	18–20
Scabiosa species PINCUSHION FLOWER	10–15	6–8	A	B	10–15
Sedum species STONECROP	15–30	6–8	—	B	6–8
Sempervivum species LIVE-FOREVER	15–30	6–8	—	B	4–8
Senecio species DUSTY-MILLER	10–15	8–10	A	B	8–10
Stokesia laevis STOKES' ASTER	25–30	8–10	A	B	12–15
Thalictrum aquilegifolium MEADOW RUE	15–30	8–10	I	B	12–18
Tradescantia species SPIDERWORT	25–30	8–10	A	B	12–15
Trillium ovatum WAKE-ROBIN	180+	—	I	—	10–12
Trollius europaeus GLOBEFLOWER	5–60+	—	I	—	8–10

PERENNIALS Species	Germination time in days	Indoor sowing — number of weeks before transplanting outdoors	Outdoor sowing — number of weeks before last frost	Outdoor transplanting — number of weeks before last frost	Planting distance in inches
Veronica species VERONICA, SPEEDWELL	15–20	6–8	A	B	12–15
Viola species VIOLA, VIOLET	10–20	8–10	G	B	6–8

Key:

A Sow outdoors from early spring through summer up until two months before first fall frost.

B Plant outdoors from early spring through summer up until two months before first fall frost.

C Sow outdoors in early spring.

D Sow outdoors in fall or early spring.

E Sow outdoors in late spring or early summer.

F Plant outdoors in early to midspring.

G Sow outdoors in fall or from early spring through summer up until two months before first fall frost.

H Sow outdoors in spring after danger of frost has passed.

I Sow outdoors in fall.

J Sow outdoors in fall, spring, or early summer.

Abelmoschus esculentus OKRA	10–14		last frost	last frost	15–18
Allium Ampeloprasum LEEK	10–14	4–6	—	4–6	6–8
Allium Cepa ONION	10–14	10–12	6–8	4–6	6–8
Apium graveolens CELERY	21–25	8–10	last frost	last frost	10–12
Asparagus officinalis ASPARAGUS	14–21	10–12	last frost	last frost	12–15
Beta vulgaris SWISS CHARD	7–10	12–14	4–6	—	6–8
Beta vulgaris BEET	10–14	—	4–6*	—	4–6
Brassica juncea MUSTARD	9–12	—	4–6*	—	6–8
Brassica Napus RUTABAGA	7–10	—	early summer	—	6–8
Brassica oleracea KALE, COLLARDS	10–14	—	4–6	4–6	12–15
Brassica oleracea CAULIFLOWER	8–10	4–6	—	2	18–24
Brassica oleracea CABBAGE	10–14	5–7	—	4–6	15–18
Brassica oleracea BRUSSELS SPROUTS	10–14	5–7	early summer	early summer	18–24
Brassica oleracea KOHLRABI	12–15	8–10	4–6	4–6	6–8
Brassica oleracea BROCCOLI	10–14	3–4	—	2	18–24
Brassica Rapa CHINESE CABBAGE	10–14	5–7	early summer	early summer	12–18
Brassica Rapa TURNIP	7–10	4–6	4–6*	—	4–6
Capsicum annuum PEPPERS	10–12	—	—	last frost	18–24
Cicer arietinum CHICK PEA, GARBANZO BEAN	6–10	6–8	last frost	—	8–12
Cichorium Endivia ENDIVE	7–14	—	early summer	early summer	8–12
Cichorium Intybus CHICORY	7–14	6–8	3–5	3–5	6–8
Citrullus lanatus WATERMELON	5–7	4–6	last frost	last frost	24–30
Cucumis Melo MELON	5–7	3–4	last frost	last frost	15–18

VEGETABLES Species	Germination time in days	Indoor sowing — number of weeks before transplanting outdoors	Outdoor sowing — number of weeks before last frost	Outdoor transplanting — number of weeks before last frost	Planting distance in inches
Cucumis sativus CUCUMBER	7–10	3–4	last frost	last frost	12–15
Cucurbita species SQUASH, PUMPKIN	7–10	4–6	last frost	last frost	24–48
Cynara Scolymus ARTICHOKE	12–15	3–4	—	last frost	36–48
Daucus Carota CARROT	14–21	6–8	4–6*	—	2–4
Glycine Max SOYBEAN	12–15	—	last frost	—	4–6
Lactuca sativa LETTUCE, LEAF	7–10	—	4–6*	4–6*	6–12
LETTUCE, HEAD	7–10	4–5	4–6	4–6	10–12
Lycopersicon Lycopersicum TOMATO	5–8	8–10	—	last frost	18–24
Pastinaca sativa PARSNIP	21–25	5–7	6–8	—	3–4
Phaseolus limensis LIMA BEAN	7–10	—	last frost	last frost	4–8
Phaseolus vulgaris GREEN BEAN	6–10	3–4	last frost*	—	3–8
Pisum sativum PEA	7–10	—	6–8*	—	2–3
Raphanus sativus RADISH	4–6	—	6–8*	—	1–2
Solanum Melongena EGGPLANT	10–15	8–10	—	last frost	24–30
Spinacia oleracea SPINACH	8–10	—	6–8*	—	4–6
Tetragonia tetragonioides NEW ZEALAND SPINACH	8–10	—	—	last frost	15–18
Vigna unguiculata COWPEA	7–10	4–5	last frost	—	3–4
Zea Mays CORN	5–7	—	last frost	—	10–14

*Make successive sowings or plantings every 2 weeks.

Anethum graveolens DILL	21–25		4–6	—	8–12
Anthriscus Cerefolium CHERVIL	7–14	—	4–6	—	8–10
Borago officinalis BORAGE	7–10	—	6–8	last frost	10–12
Carthamus tinctorius SAFFLOWER	10–14	6–8	last frost	last frost	10–12
Coriandrum sativum CORIANDER	10–14	—	4–6	last frost	8–10
Cuminum Cyminum CUMIN	10–14	6–8	last frost	—	20–24
Eruca vesicaria ROCKET	5–8	—	4–6	—	12–14
Foeniculum species FENNEL	10–14	—	last frost	—	8–12
Matricaria recutita CHAMOMILE	10–12	—	4–6	4–6	6–12
Ocimum Basilicuum BASIL	7–10	4–6	last frost	last frost	10–12
Origanum Majorana MARJORAM	8–14	6–8	4–6	4–6	6–8
Petroselinum crispum PARSLEY	14–21	6–8	2–4	—	6–8
Pimpinella Anisum ANISE	18–20	—	last frost	—	6–8
Satureja hortensis SUMMER SAVORY	10–15	—	—	last frost	8–12
Sesamum indicum SESAME	5–7	6–8	last frost	—	8–10

Species	Germination time in days	Indoor sowing — number of weeks before transplanting outdoors	Outdoor sowing — number of weeks before last frost	Outdoor transplanting — number of weeks before last frost	Planting distance in inches
PERENNIAL AND BIENNIAL HERBS					
Allium Schoenoprasum CHIVES	10-14	—	4-6	4-6	6-8
Angelica Archangelica ANGELICA	21-25	6-8	late fall	4-6	24-36
Artemisia Dracunculus SIBERIAN TARRAGON	20-25	6-8	4-6	2-4	15-18
Carum Carvi CARAWAY	10-14	6-8	late fall	—	10-12
Hyssopus officinalis HYSSOP	7-10	—	4-6	4-6	15-18
Lavandula angustifolia LAVENDER	15-20	6-8	6-8	4-6	10-12
Levisticum officinale LOVAGE	10-14	6-8	late fall	4-6	30-36
Marrubium vulgare HOREHOUND	10-14	6-8	6-8	—	12-15
Melissa officinalis LEMON BALM	14-16	—	4-6	4-6	10-12
Mentha species MINT	12-16	6-8	4-6	4-6	10-12
Nasturtium officinale WATERCRESS	7-10	6-8	4-6	2-4	3-4
Nepeta species CATMINT	7-10	6-8	4-6	4-6	6-15
Poterium Sanguisorba BURNET	8-10	6-8	2-4	2-4	12-15
Rosmarinus officinalis ROSEMARY	18-21	6-8	4-6	4-6	12-18
Ruta graveolens RUE	10-14	6-8	4-6	4-6	6-12
Salvia officinalis SAGE	14-21	6-8	4-6	4-6	12-18
Satureja montana WINTER SAVORY	15-20	6-8	—	last frost	12-15
Thymus species THYME	21-30	6-8	4-6	4-6	6-8

NOTE: For some herbs it is not recommended to start plants indoors, but this may nevertheless be accomplished successfully if you sow into individual pots to eliminate transplant shock. Star, the seeds indoors 6–8 weeks before transplanting outside.